OUR
TEJANO HEROES

OUR
TEJANO HEROES
Outstanding Mexican-Americans in Texas

SAMMYE MUNSON

PANDA BOOKS   ★   **Austin, Texas**

Published in the United States of America
By Panda Books
An Imprint of Eakin Publications, Inc.
P.O. Drawer 90159   ★   Austin, Texas 78709-0159

ISBN 0-89015-691-3

Library of Congress Cataloging-in-Publication Data

Munson, Sammye.
    Our Tejano heroes : outstanding Mexican-Americans in Texas / Sammye
Munson.
        p.   cm.
    Bibliography: p.
    Summary: Examines the accomplishments and contributions of thirty sig-
nificant Mexican-Americans in Texas, including historic figures such as Jose
Antonio Navarro and contemporary people such as Congressman Henry B.
Gonzalez.
    ISBN 0-89015-691-3 : $9.95
        1. Mexican-Americans — Texas — Biography — Juvenile literature.
    2. Texas — Biography — Juvenile literature. [1. Mexican-Americans-
Texas. 2. Texas — Biography.] I. Title.
F395.M5M86   1989
920'.009268720764--dc19
[B]
[92]   88-32461
                                                                  CIP
                                                                   AC

Dedicated to Leslie,
for his patience and support

Contents

Acknowledgments

I am deeply grateful to the libraries in Texas that have given me help in writing this book. Special thanks goes to Dr. Tom Kreneck, archivist at the Houston Public Library. I also appreciate the help of Tom Shelton, librarian of the Institute of Texan Cultures. Thanks to Texas Woman's University Library, Denton; Barker Texas History Center in Austin; Texas A&I University; and the Tomás Rivera Archive, University of California, Riverside.

Introduction

A *Tejano* (tay **hah** no) is a person who lives in Texas but whose family once came from Mexico. A *Tejano* is also called a Mexican-American.

Tejanos lived in Texas long before Texas was a state. For many years, Texas was a part of Mexico. When Texas citizens wanted to be free of Mexico's rule, heroes like Juan Seguin and Gregorio Esparza fought bravely for Texas's independence.

Later, Lorenzo de Zavala and Antonio Navarro helped set up the republic's first government. For many years since, Mexican-Americans have played a big part in developing the state.

The hot, parched ground of the cotton fields was home to some of these people. They worked as migrant workers when they were children. They followed the crops when the cotton or vegetables were ready to be picked. This meant missing a great deal of school.

Tomás Rivera and Patrick Flores were among the children who labored under the blistering sun. They could have dropped out of school. But Rivera went on to become a writer, teacher, and poet. Patrick Flores struggled to get an education and became the first Mexican-American archbishop in the Catholic Church.

The *Tejanos* featured in this book come from different areas of the state. All have different backgrounds. They are war heroes, statesmen, doctors, and business people.

It would be impossible to include all the *Tejanos* who have made important contributions to the state. These few are representative of the many who have achieved so much.

While interviewing many of these people and reading about their lives, I was deeply moved. I admire them because they overcame poverty and prejudice to become leaders in their fields. I hope that you, too, will be proud and grateful for their lives.

Pronunciation Key

Candalaria	Kon dah **lah** ree ah
De Zavala	Day Sah **vah** la
Seguin	Say **geen**
Esparza	Ays **par** sah
Navarro	Nah **var** ō
Benavidez	Ben ah **vee** des
Cavazos	Cah **vah** sōs
Cisneros	Sees **neh** rōs
Flores	**Floor** es
Garcia	Gar **see** ah
Garza	**Gar** sah
Gonzalez	Gōn **sah** les
Laurenzo	Lah **ren** zo
Mendoza	Men **dō** sah
Rangel	Rahn **hel**
Rivera	Ree **ver** ah
Trevino	Trah **veen** yo
Tenayuca	Ten ah **you** cah
Tijerina	Tee her **ree** nah

Andrea Castanon Ramirez Candalaria

Nurse of the Alamo

We usually think of brave men fighting for Texas's freedom when we remember the Battle of the Alamo. History tells us that there was also a brave woman present who survived the battle. She lived to be 113 years old.

Andrea Castanon Ramirez Candalaria was born in Nuevo Laredo, Mexico, but moved to Laredo, Texas, when she was a little girl. When she was twenty-five years old, she moved to San Antonio.

Señora Candalaria said that she nursed wounded men during the battle. During the twelve-day siege of the Alamo, men were dying around her. She took care of them and made their last hours as comfortable as possible.

One of the men she took care of was James Bowie, second-in-command at the Alamo. Bowie was very ill with a high fever. He was weak and coughed constantly as the battle raged.

Candalaria said that Bowie died the day before the Alamo was captured. The Mexican soldiers stormed into the mission to take the dead men's bodies and burn them. Candalaria begged the soldiers to allow Bowie's body to be buried instead of burned. She told them he had died from an illness, not from the battle.

The Mexican soldiers thought that Bowie was still alive and that Candalaria was trying to trick them. One of them pulled a sword and stabbed Bowie. Since Candalaria was standing over Bowie to protect him, she was wounded by the sword. She was cut on the chin and wrist

1

Madame Candalaria with James Bowie at the Alamo.
— Institute of Texan Cultures, San Antonio

and bore the scars until her death. Bowie's body, however, was burned along with the other Texans who gave their lives at the Alamo.

Candalaria was one of thirteen women and children who survived the Battle of the Alamo. She was also a heroine during the terrible smallpox epidemic. She nursed those who had the dreaded disease without regard or fear for her own life.

She had four children of her own but adopted twenty-two orphans during her long life. She remained in San Antonio, where she lived a quiet life and enjoyed telling others of her interesting experiences.

When Candalaria was 106 years old, the State of Texas decided to give her a monthly pension of twelve dollars per month for her devotion to others at the Alamo and during the smallpox epidemic.

She lived seven more years before dying in San Antonio. We remember Andrea Castanon Ramirez Candalaria as one of the bravest women in Texas.

Lorenzo de Zavala

Designer of the First Texas Flag

Lorenzo de Zavala, early hero of both Mexico and Texas, was born in Tecoh, a village in Yucatán, Mexico. Since Lorenzo was a good student and eager to learn, his parents sent him to a boardingschool.

The Franciscan priests at the school were excellent teachers. Lorenzo studied a variety of subjects, including philosophy, Latin, French, and mathematics. His main interests were in law and politics.

Lorenzo completed his studies in four years. He wanted to go to Mexico City to study law, but the lack of money kept him from going. Instead, he returned to his village at the age of nineteen and became active in trading and politics.

Lorenzo always believed that people should be free and should govern themselves. Spain ruled Mexico in those days and did not allow the people to govern. Lorenzo thought that Yucatán should be free of Spanish rule. He wrote many articles about his views. The displeased Spaniards sent him to prison for three years.

He did not waste these years but spent them in study. He read many books, including some about medicine. He also learned to speak English. When he finally was freed and returned home, there was a terrible cholera epidemic. His knowledge of medicine was useful in treating the sick people.

Mexico had declared independence from Spain by this time, and Lorenzo was on his way to becoming a leader of his people. He was chosen to serve in the National Congress in Mexico City. He also helped write the new constitution for his country.

Because he believed in the rights of all people, he was elected as governor of the state of Mexico. Lorenzo was a successful governor. He started the first state library, built schools and factories, and received a land grant that would allow 500 Mexican families to settle in Texas.

Some of the leaders in Mexico did not agree with Lorenzo's beliefs. They did not want people to govern themselves. And they disagreed with Lorenzo's idea that Texas should be independent. These leaders, called Centralists, became powerful and forced Lorenzo to resign as governor.

Later, the Centralists lost their power and Lorenzo regained his position as governor. He was even given the job of minister of the treasury. He had the responsibility

Lorenzo de Zavala
— Senate Chamber, Texas State
Capitol, Austin

5

of handling the state's money. Again, though, the Centralists became powerful and put Lorenzo out of office.

After losing his jobs in the government, Lorenzo traveled in the United States. He met many important people, including President John Quincy Adams. He also visited France, where he wrote articles about the Mexican revolutions.

Santa Anna, the new president of Mexico, appointed Lorenzo minister to France. At first Lorenzo admired Santa Anna. Then he realized that the president really wanted to become a dictator and take away the people's rights.

Lorenzo wanted nothing more to do with Santa Anna. He resigned his position with the Mexican government. Then he and his family moved to Texas and built a home near Houston on Buffalo Bayou.

The people in Texas were ruled by Mexico at this time but wanted to be independent. Lorenzo agreed with them. "Fight for your rights; resist Santa Anna," he told them.

Since Lorenzo had been a leader in the Mexican government, he was respected by the Texans. They listened to what he told them. Stephen F. Austin, the Texas leader, had been put in prison in Mexico City. When he returned to Texas, he met with Lorenzo and wanted his advice.

In 1836 Lorenzo met with fifty-six Texans and two other Mexican-Americans to sign the Texas Declaration of Independence. Lorenzo was everyone's choice for vice-president of the Republic of Texas.

Lorenzo then became involved in planning a defense against Mexico. Santa Anna heard of the plans and tried to capture the Texas leaders. Lorenzo and others escaped to Harrisburg, then went on to Galveston.

Santa Anna camped at San Jacinto to await the rest of his army. General Sam Houston surprised the Mexican forces there and defeated them on April 21, 1836.

Lorenzo was not well. He returned to his home on

Buffalo Bayou to rest. At this time he designed the first flag of Texas. It was blue with a gold star in the center. The word "TEXAS" was written around the star. This flag was later replaced with the one we use today.

Lorenzo tried to continue his duties as vice-president, but he was not well enough. One day he decided to take his young son for a boat ride on Buffalo Bayou. A strong wind began blowing, and the boat overturned. Lorenzo, thinking only of his son, rescued the boy and swam to shore with him. The boy was fine, but the experience was too much for Lorenzo. He developed pneumonia and died at his home a short time later.

Lorenzo de Zavala was a gentleman, a scholar, and a leader who believed that citizens should have the right to freedom and a part of the governing process. He lived his life according to these beliefs. Texas was fortunate to have him as a leader.

Erasmo and Juan Seguin

Early Texas Heroes

Erasmo and Juan Seguin were a father and son who helped make Texas free. They were both native Texans, born in San Antonio.

Erasmo, the father, became a leader of the town. He was mayor, postmaster, and started one of the first schools. He was also a successful rancher and farmer. He developed new ways of growing cotton.

But we remember him most as a hero in early Texas. He believed that Texas should be free of Mexico's rule. He taught his son, Juan, to believe in freedom too.

Erasmo, a friend of Stephen F. Austin's, helped the Texas soldiers in many ways. He gave them food to eat and horses to ride. Because Erasmo was so helpful, he was chosen to attend the Convention of 1836. This was a meeting held to discuss the future of Texas. Erasmo became ill, however, and could not attend.

Juan was much like his father. He was a leader who had strong beliefs. When Juan was twelve years old, his father gave him a horse of his own. Juan named her Reina (Princess). From that day on, Juan loved horses.

Three years later, when Juan was almost fifteen, his father asked him to go to Nacogdoches on an important mission. They were to meet a group of new settlers and lead them to their new home in San Antonio.

Juan learned much on that trip. He met Stephen F. Austin and other leaders. He listened to adults talking about events in Mexico and in Texas. He learned that Mexico had won independence from Spain. He also heard of a new leader in Mexico named Santa Anna.

Several years later, Juan took over the family ranch when his father became postmaster. He then married his childhood sweetheart, Gertrudis.

Juan heard that Santa Anna was sending soldiers to San Antonio. He talked with Stephen Austin and agreed that Texas should be free of Mexico's rule. Austin asked Juan to lead a group of men to watch for Santa Anna's army. General Cos was leading the Mexican army.

Finally, General Cos and his men arrived with their cannons. Juan and his men hid inside an old church. Each time one of the Mexican soldiers started to fire the cannon, the Texans shot them with rifles. They put the rifles through holes in the walls of the church.

The small group of Texas men under Juan Seguin were able to keep the soldiers from destroying the church. Finally, the Mexican army left. About sixty of them had been killed, while only one Texan had lost his life.

But General Cos and his army were not giving up so

Juan Seguin
— Texas State Library, Austin

9

easily. The people in San Antonio were afraid. Juan felt sorry for his friends. They believed in freedom, but they also feared for their lives.

When he was sure the Mexican army was on its way, Juan sent his family to Nacogdoches for safety. He heard that an old mission called the Alamo was going to be used as a fort. He rode his horse to the gates of the building.

Davy Crockett and his men arrived to prepare for the battle. The Texans knew that General Cos and his men were nearby. They warned the townspeople of the coming battle. Some of them rushed into the walls of the Alamo for safety.

Then the Mexican cannons began firing. In a short time they surrounded the Alamo. The small force of Texas soldiers needed more men and ammunition. Six days of fighting passed.

Colonel William B. Travis gathered his men together. "We must have help. Someone must go to Fannin and ask him for guns and men."

"I will go," said Captain Juan Seguin.

"It is a dangerous mission, and we need you here," Colonel Travis replied.

"I speak Spanish and have a good chance of getting through enemy lines. I am the one to go," Juan said.

That evening Juan and his aide left the Alamo at sunset. It was a long ride to see James W. Fannin at Goliad. The night ride was dangerous, but the men rode as far as they could. They stopped to rest awhile and began their trip at dawn the next morning.

Before they arrived in the town, they learned that Fannin had already sent men and guns. However, the wagons had broken down and the group had to turn back. Juan also learned that Fannin was preparing for a battle at Goliad. He could spare no men or guns.

Juan and his aide rode on in hopes of seeing General Sam Houston. When they found him, General Houston did offer help. He sent men and supplies.

As they neared San Antonio, Juan was worried. He

10

heard no gunfire. Then he saw black smoke in the sky. The supplies and men had come too late. The Alamo had fallen.

Juan was very sad. But he wasn't going to give up. He led a group of soldiers on horseback in the Battle of San Jacinto.

After the war was over, Juan went to his family in Nacogdoches. They were almost starved and sick, but he helped them return to their home in San Antonio.

He was very sad that the bodies of the Alamo heroes had been burned without a proper funeral. He arranged a burial for their ashes and gave a speech in their behalf.

Juan was popular with the people in San Antonio. They elected him their mayor in 1841.

On a trip to Mexico he discovered that the Mexican government was planning to invade the city again. Juan returned to warn the Texas government. But a Mexican commander spread the lie that Juan had helped the Mexican forces. He and other Mexicans were forced to leave San Antonio. Juan was arrested by Mexican officials and thrown into prison. Santa Anna forced him to fight with his army.

Later, Juan lived in both Texas and in Mexico. During the last part of his life, he was considered to be a traitor. He died in 1890.

History later proved that the accusations were false. Juan came to be known as a true Texas patriot. He fought bravely for his state and helped it gain independence.

The town of Seguin is named in honor of Juan and his father, Erasmo. Juan was buried in Nuevo Laredo. But during the United States Bicentennial in 1976, his body was moved to its present grave in Seguin.

The Gregorio Esparza Family
Defenders of the Alamo

Gregorio Esparza was one of nine Mexican-Americans to fight and die at the Alamo. He even fought against his own brother because he believed in freedom for Texas.

Gregorio and his brother, Francisco, were born in San Antonio. Each had different ideas about government. Gregorio fought with the Texas army, and Francisco fought with the Mexican army.

Texas was still a part of Mexico in 1835. Mexico was ruled by Santa Anna, who was a dictator. He believed that the people should do as he said. Gregorio believed that people should have the right to vote and express themselves. He wanted Texas to be free of Mexico's rule.

Santa Anna sent his brother-in-law, General Cos, to San Antonio to capture the city. But the Texas army was strong enough to defeat the Mexicans. Gregorio fought in this battle.

Losing the battle made Santa Anna very angry. He promised he would teach the Texans a lesson. The Texans heard he wanted revenge. They heard he was sending another army to take over the city.

Gregorio wanted his wife and four children to leave San Antonio before a battle began. A wagon was supposed to get them and take them to Nacogdoches. But the wagon did not arrive in time.

"What shall we do, Father?" asked Enrique, Gregorio's eight-year-old son.

"You will go to the Alamo with me," Gregorio told his wife and children. "You will be safe within its thick walls."

The Alamo was a mission that was being used as a

Gregorio and Enrique Esparza
— Institute of Texan Cultures,
San Antonio

13

fort. The Esparzas packed a few belongings and hurried to the Alamo. It was almost dark when they arrived. The gates were closed and barred.

Gregorio called to the guard, and Enrique beat his fists against the wall to get attention. Finally, a guard heard them.

"I will help you climb over the wall," he said.

Gregorio helped his wife and children over the wall. Then he climbed over too. It was well past dark when they were safely inside and settled.

Since it was late, the three younger children went to sleep. But Enrique could not sleep. He thought this was an exciting adventure. He did not know what was in store for them the following day.

The next morning everyone was up early. Gregorio had to report for duty at his cannon on top of the Alamo's walls.

When they heard cannons fire from outside, they knew that Santa Anna was attacking. Colonel James W. Bowie told the Texas soldiers that anyone who wished to leave could do so.

"No, I will stay and die fighting, I am not afraid," Gregorio told him.

The cannons roared day and night. Enrique was afraid for his father's life. Since Gregorio could not leave his cannon, the boy brought him food and talked to him.

Day after day the battle continued. The soldiers, including Gregorio, were very tired. Still, they fought bravely.

Finally, the guns were silent. Santa Anna's army broke into the walls of the Alamo. Many of the soldiers had already been killed. But Santa Anna gave an order that anyone still alive should be killed.

After thirteen days of fighting, the Texans lost. They had great courage, but the Mexican army outnumbered them.

Enrique was very sad. He knew his father had died.

His Uncle Francisco was sad too. Santa Anna then said that all the bodies of the soldiers were to be burned.

Francisco was very upset that his brother would not have a proper burial. He begged for permission to bury his dead brother. Santa Anna finally agreed. Francisco and Enrique began the search for Gregorio's body.

They took a lantern to help them find the body. They found it in a small chapel in the building. Gregorio had a cannon ball in his chest and a sword wound in his side.

Francisco saw to it that his brother's body was buried. Gregorio was the only Texas soldier to have a burial.

The rest of the Esparza family and about eight other people lived through the ordeal. Enrique lived to be eighty-nine years old. He never forgot his experiences at the Alamo. He was proud that his father gave his life fighting for freedom in Texas.

José Antonio Navarro

Signer of Texas Declaration of Independence

José Antonio Navarro helped make important decisions for Texas for fifty years. He was born in San Antonio when Texas was still a part of Mexico.

As a boy, José loved horses. One day he was thrown from his horse. The horse fell on his leg, injuring it badly. From that time on, José walked with a limp.

He never let his physical handicap keep him from leading a full, productive life. He was a tall man, muscular and strong. Since there were no schools in San Antonio in those days, José educated himself by reading books. He did spend one year in a college at Saltillo, Mexico. His main interest was in law. He became an expert in land matters and in constitutional law. This knowledge helped him write laws for Texas.

He married when he was about thirty years old. In three years he was elected to the legislature of Texas and Coahuila. He worked in the family store and was also a rancher. Since he owned land in five counties, he probably owned more land than any other person at that time in Texas.

Although he was busy with the family business and with ranching, he still devoted time to government service. At that time Mexico was still under the control of Spain. José took an active part in helping Mexico win her independence from Spain. During the struggle, he had to leave Texas and hide in Louisiana. Finally, when Mexico broke from Spain's rule, José returned to his home.

He then played a role in Texas government. In 1829 he created a law that gave land to the Texas settlers. Families who agreed to build homes and plant crops were entitled to receive the land. This later became the Homestead Law.

A few years later, Navarro became active in Texas's fight for independence from Mexico. He talked with Stephen F. Austin many times, offering his advice and help. Navarro felt that Texas should be free of Mexico's rule and that all people should be free and equal.

In 1836 important leaders of Texas met to decide Texas's fate. Navarro was present at the meeting and signed the Texas Declaration of Independence. After Texas won independence, he helped with the organization of the government.

With his knowledge of law, he helped write the Texas Constitution. He also served in the Third Congress of the Republic of Texas.

The president of Texas, Mirabeau Lamar, urged Navarro to join a committee that would lead 320 men into Santa Fe, New Mexico. The purpose of the journey was to persuade Santa Fe to become part of Texas.

José Antonio Navarro
— Library, Daughters of Republic of
Texas, San Antonio

Navarro, always loyal, consented. But the Santa Fe Expedition ended in disaster. The group was arrested by Mexican soldiers as soon as it arrived. The soldiers then made the prisoners walk to Mexico City, a distance of 2,000 miles.

Although their shoes were worn thin, and they had only crusts of bread to eat each day, they walked through city after city. Navarro's leg, which he injured as a child, became swollen and inflamed. He begged for mercy and was allowed to ride in a donkey cart for part of the way.

All the men were finally freed, except for Navarro. The Mexican government considered him a traitor since he had defended Texas during the war. Santa Anna sentenced him to death but changed the sentence to life imprisonment.

Navarro served more than three years in jail. He would have spent the rest of his life in prison except for a lucky incident. An American was visiting the prison, saw his plight, and helped him escape. Navarro returned to San Antonio, a hero.

On his return, he added a new symbol to the brand on his cattle. The brand showed a line and circle, a symbol of the leg irons Navarro wore in prison.

He was surprised to learn that while he was gone, Texas was considering becoming part of the United States. He again offered his skills and helped to write the new state constitution. He was also elected state senator in the first and second legislatures.

Navarro gradually retired from politics and spent his time managing his ranches and his store. He built a stone house in San Antonio, where he died in 1871. His house has been restored and made a state historical site.

Some years before Navarro died, the state legislature named a new county after him. He was given the honor of naming the county seat of Navarro County. He named it Corsicana in memory of his father's birthplace, on the Isle of Corsica. A bronze statue of José Navarro was erected in front of the courthouse in Corsicana, Texas.

José Antonio Navarro was a quiet man whose service and loyalty to Texas helped make the state great.

Roy Benavidez

War Hero

Duty. Honor. Country. Roy Benavidez first heard these words when he was thirteen or fourteen years old. They impressed him and changed his life. The three words made Roy realize he wanted to make his life count for something. He wanted to be a soldier, perhaps a paratrooper.

Roy remembered the three words when he landed in the jungles of Vietnam. He thought of them as he risked his life to save the lives of eight American soldiers.

Roy's parents died when he was a young boy. He went to live with an aunt and uncle in El Campo. Roy was not much of a student and dropped out of school in the seventh grade. Since he had little education or training, he joined migrant workers, traveling and picking vegetables.

Roy's goal was still to become a soldier. When he was seventeen, he joined the National Guard. At eighteen he went into the U.S. Army. He was sent to Korea and Germany but saw little action.

Roy was sent to Vietnam when the war began. He was hit by a land mine and was paralyzed. The doctor gave him little hope of ever walking. But Roy was determined. He suffered through much pain as he taught himself to walk again.

Roy did not want a medical discharge. He still wanted to serve his country. He wanted to be a paratrooper. The training was difficult, but he knew he could do it.

In his training he had to run four miles with a forty-pound backpack, then do exercises. He had to endure twelve days in a forest with little food or water and find his way back. It was especially hard for him because of his earlier injuries. When he wasn't training, he was studying difficult material.

Roy was accepted into the Green Berets, the best fighting group in the country. He was proud to wear the uniform and proud to be a part of that group.

Finally, the day came when his courage and training were put to the test. He jumped from a helicopter into the jungles of Vietnam. He was to rescue American soldiers and save important papers.

Roy was shot in the leg immediately, but he ignored the pain and went on to do his duty. He used the medical supplies he had thrown from the helicopter to aid the soldiers.

He was shot in the thigh as he worked. Still he didn't give up. When a bullet pierced his back, he did not know if he could continue. But he went on, enduring terrible pain as he helped his fellow soldiers.

Rockets and bullets were falling around him. Roy's body was dripping with blood and he was dizzy as he worked. He lifted heavy men, carrying or dragging them to the helicopter. When he met an enemy soldier, face-to-face, the man hit him over the head with the butt of his gun. Then he smashed Roy's mouth with the gun. Roy was stunned, but with almost super-human strength, he subdued the man.

Roy made three trips carrying the men to safety. Finally, he was helped into the helicopter and flown to a

Roy Benavidez

hospital in Saigon. His arm, legs, back, head, and face suffered terrible injuries.

Roy spent most of the year recovering in the hospital. His wife Lala and other family members visited when they could. While in the hospital, Roy was awarded the Purple Heart and the Distinguished Service Cross, the second highest honor a fighting man can receive.

After he left the hospital, he stayed in the army but was no longer able to be a paratrooper. He was assigned various duties, including driving cars for generals.

In 1976 Sergeant Benavidez retired from the army. He had served his country for twenty years and three months. And he had almost given his life to save eight American soldiers.

Roy returned to his family in El Campo. Four years later, he received the Medal of Honor for his courage as a U.S. fighting man. This is the highest award a soldier can receive. It was an inspirational day as Sergeant Benavidez accepted the award from President Ronald Reagan, with his wife and son looking on.

Although he dropped out of school in the seventh grade, Roy has since gotten his high school diploma and finished two years of college. He is unable to work because of his war injuries but spends time talking to students and other groups.

Roy believes in his country and is not ashamed to tell others how he feels. He wants people to respect the American flag and be proud of it. He also speaks of the value of education. He wants students to know how important it is to stay in school and get an education.

Duty. Honor. Country. Only three little words, but words that made Sergeant Roy Benavidez a hero in the United States.

The Cavazos Family

Triumphs of a Texas Family

Five Cavazos children grew up on the famous King Ranch in South Texas. The rough land was sometimes cruel, sometimes kind. But each of the children gained something from the experience. They learned to love the outdoors and to overcome obstacles in order to succeed.

Lauro F. Cavazos, Sr., and his wife Tomasa taught their children to value education. They also believed their children could achieve any goal if they worked hard enough.

Father Lauro was foreman of the Santa Gertrudis section of the King Ranch for more than forty years. He helped develop the first American breed of cattle, the Santa Gertrudis.

Lauro was a hard-working man who started at the ranch when he was eighteen years old. He lived and worked on the ranch until his death in 1958. He left only once, to serve in World War I.

Lauro took an active part in the last major Texas gunfight. When a group of bandits invaded the ranch, he and a few other men fought off the attackers.

He had high standards for his family. He wanted each of them to get an education and for his sons to serve in the military. He got his wish. All five of his children graduated from college, and his sons served their country in several wars.

Tomasa also had a great influence on their children. She was a gentle woman who taught them to love life and respect others.

Their only daughter, Sarita (now Mrs. Albert Ochoa), credits her parents and early teachers for the successes that she and her brothers have had. She recalls

The Cavazos family: General Richard Cavazos, Dr. Lauro F. Cavazos, Joseph A. Cavazos, Sarita Ochoa, and Robert Cavazos with mother, Tomasa Cavazos.

that her father bought a house in town so that the children could go to good schools. At one time she was the only Mexican-American in an all-white school.

Sarita has been a successful home economics teacher. She is also known for her cooking skills. She often volunteers her talents for fund-raising events in Laredo. At one time she had a television program on cooking.

Living on the large King Ranch was an adventure to five children. Each of the sons became good horsemen and learned to deal with any crisis that occurred.

The first son of the family, Lauro F. Cavazos, Jr., enlisted in the army when he was only seventeen. After serving, he enrolled at Texas Tech University. He received a bachelor's and master's degree in zoology. Money was scarce, but he managed to earn two degrees.

The younger Lauro then went to the University of Iowa and received his doctoral degree. He became a college professor and taught science courses. Tufts University School of Medicine recognized his gifts and made him associate dean of the medical school. Later, he was chosen dean of Tufts Medical School.

In 1980 Dr. Cavazos became president of Texas Tech. His ability as a scientist and teacher is highly respected. He has done research on many scientific subjects and has written more than seventy-five articles dealing with biology or medical education. He also has been editor of several medical journals.

Dr. Cavazos has been active in many health organizations and has contributed to health education. In 1984 President Ronald Reagan presented him the award for Outstanding Leadership in the Field of Education. A few years later, Reagan selected Cavazos to serve as the nation's secretary of education.

Richard, the second son in the family, learned honesty, discipline, and bravery as he grew up on the ranch. He became an expert marksman as he shot rattlesnakes and hunted animals. This experience served him well in later years. He became the first Mexican-American four-star general in the United States.

Richard was a good athlete. He was captain of the Kingsville High School football team and was one of the first Mexican-Americans to play football for Texas Tech University. He was a leader in school as much as on the football field.

He liked growing up on the King Ranch. Although the family had little money, there was plenty of love. Dealing with the challenges of the rugged land made him a stronger person.

Richard began his studies at Texas Tech University, planning to major in geology. He had not thought of making the military a career. But when he went into the army after graduating from college, he became an outstanding soldier.

Because of his service, he was the first Mexican-American to become a four-star general. Perhaps his father's desire to see his sons serve their country influenced him.

General Cavazos was a war hero whose courage earned him respect and many honors. In 1953 he crossed a hill in Korea to rescue five wounded men. Although the enemy was nearby, he helped the men to safety. Wounded himself, he returned twice to help others reach safety.

This example of courage earned him the Distinguished Service Cross. He won this award later in Vietnam. He also received the Silver Star, Legion of Merit, Distinguished Flying Cross, Bronze Star, and Purple Heart.

Before his retirement from the army, General Cavazos was in charge of the U.S. Army Command at Fort McPherson, Georgia. This is the headquarters of 380,000 regular army troops and 600,000 National Guardsmen.

His successful career went beyond even his father's dream for his son. In 1984 the city of Kingsville named a street in his honor, General Cavazos Boulevard.

General Richard Cavazos

Dr. Lauro F. Cavazos

Another son, Robert (Bobby), had his father's love for the ranch. He liked the life of a cowboy and the challenges it offered. He worked at the ranch during summers, herding cattle while riding horseback.

Bobby also attended Texas Tech University and became a well-known football star. He was the only player to make the first-team All Border Conference three years straight. He set a standard as a running back at the university. He was also a popular leader on campus during his college days.

After graduation, he was selected to play for a professional football team in Chicago. A broken shoulder ended his career, however. He then became an officer in the army and served in the Korean War. Today Bobby is in business in Corpus Christi.

The youngest member of the family, Joe, graduated from St. Mary's University in San Antonio. He is a successful businessman in Bossier City, Louisiana. He manages of one of the largest department stores in the city and has won awards for his work.

The Cavazos family of Kingsville is one of the state's outstanding families. Its members have lived under five of the six flags of Texas. They continue to make important contributions to the state.

Henry Cisneros

Leader of San Antonio

When Henry Cisneros was a small boy, he spent many hours at his grandfather's print shop. He often met leaders of the community there. He heard them discuss ideas that were important to the people of San Antonio.

Henry listened and learned. He became aware of the importance of good government. Perhaps he even dreamed of someday becoming a leader.

Henry grew up with two sisters and one brother. His childhood was filled with fun. There were many children in the neighborhood. After a day at school, he played baseball or football with friends.

Yet Henry's parents were strict with their children. They wanted each one to be a good student and to develop his or her talents. Television was allowed only on weekends, unless the program was educational. The children read, worked with hobbies, and took music lessons. They were also expected to do their share of the household chores.

When Henry started school, his parents decided to speak English at home. They felt that this would help their children in school.

Henry has a home on the west side of San Antonio where he lived as a child. Some of his fondest memories are of the Sundays he stayed with his grandparents. After church the entire family would spend the afternoon at his grandparents' home.

Sometimes Henry's grandfather would select books for Henry to read. Usually they were about Mexico. When Henry was about fifteen, and his grandfather was eighty, they visited Mexico together. His grandfather was proud of the country in which he was born. He wanted his grandson to feel the same pride.

When he was very young, Henry wanted to be an air force pilot. He joined the ROTC at Central Catholic High School in San Antonio. He learned to play the French horn in the band.

Although he yearned to be a pilot, Henry was too young at high school graduation to be admitted into the Air Force Academy. He chose to attend Texas A&M University instead. At first, he considered majoring in engineering. Later, he changed his major to city management.

In 1967 a teacher at A&M encouraged him to attend a student conference at West Point. He visited New York City at that time and was impressed with the great urban city. He began to feel that a career in city government would be a challenge. He tried even harder in school after this experience. About the time he graduated, his ambition was to someday be the mayor of San Antonio.

After college graduation, he returned to his hometown and worked in the Model Cities Program. He then entered George Washington University to pursue more education. During this time he worked at the National League of Cities and in the office of Health, Education and Welfare.

Later he went to Boston and received a master's degree in public administration at Harvard University. He married Mary Alice Perez, his high school sweetheart. They moved back to San Antonio in 1974.

The following year, at the age of twenty-seven, Henry was elected to the city council in San Antonio. In 1981 he ran for mayor and was elected. He wanted to improve the city's economy, especially through technology.

As mayor, he visited companies in other cities and told them about the business opportunities in San Antonio. Just as he set goals for himself, he set goals for his city. He helped bring about an expressway for traffic, build new bank buildings, and establish non-polluting factories.

Henry Cisneros

Citizens, both rich and poor, were happy with San Antonio's progress. In 1983 they voted to reelect Henry Cisneros as mayor.

In 1986 Walter Mondale, the Democratic candidate for president, considered Cisneros as a possible candidate for the vice-presidency of the United States.

The young, dynamic leader was elected president of the Texas Municipal League in 1984 and was also chosen the second vice-president of the National League of Cities.

Henry Cisneros believes that cities must be willing to change and grow. Since we live in an age of technology, he believes that change is the way to achieve progress.

The leadership that Henry Cisneros has shown has undoubtedly benefited San Antonio.

José Cisneros

Western Artist

The small boy took a piece of charcoal and drew a horse on the walls of his adobe home. He had no pencil or paper — only the desire to draw.

Since that day many years ago, José Cisneros has drawn hundreds of pictures of horses and the people who rode them. He knows much about how they looked.

Born in Durango, Mexico, José grew up during the Mexican Revolution. He was not able to go to school when he was very young, but he taught himself to read by sounding out the letters in words.

When his uncle found out that José could read, he

took the boy home with him and sent him to school. José was eleven years old at the time.

José spent about three years at the school. His favorite subject was history. He loved reading about the past. He also collected pictures from old newspapers and magazines. He studied the pictures and began drawing some of his own.

From his earliest years, José wanted to be an artist. But he had many obstacles in his life. He and his family had to leave their home because of the revolution. They moved to Juarez, Mexico, the city across from El Paso.

José received permission to go across the border and attend school in El Paso. He spent three years at the Lydia Patterson Institute. He learned to speak English there and he studied history. To pay his way, he swept schoolrooms and delivered newspapers.

Soon José had to drop out of school to support his family. For a while he delivered groceries. Later he was a window decorator for a department store. He saved the old pieces of cardboard from the store and used them for his artwork.

But José missed going to school. He still wanted to learn. Then he discovered the El Paso Public Library. He spent many hours there. The librarian helped him find books about history. He read them eagerly and tried to imagine how people looked long ago. He studied the works of the great artists.

Although he worked hard all day, he worked at his art at night and on weekends. He also continued reading and studying history.

Finally, some of his drawings were accepted by a magazine in Mexico City. They appeared on the covers of several magazines. José did not receive money for his work, but he was encouraged.

He married a woman named Vicente, and eventually they had five daughters. He worked to support them as well as his mother. No matter how busy he was, though, he continued drawing.

In 1959 José was hired by the El Paso Bus Company to supervise the painting of buses. He often decorated the buses with colorful designs showing the flags of Mexico and of the United States.

One day José watched the well-known painter Tom Lea at work. He showed Mr. Lea some of his own drawings. The painter was impressed with José's work and realized his great talent. He introduced him to a publisher, Carl Hertzog.

José began illustrating books for Mr. Hertzog. He was especially skillful with detailed map work and fancy lettering. José had his first art show at the El Paso Library. Since that time, his work has been shown in cities all over the United States and in Mexico.

He has also illustrated books for many other publishers. His main interest has been in the early horsemen of the Southwest. He has spent a lifetime reading about them. He knows how they looked, the kind of clothes they wore, and the types of horses they rode. He is considered to be the leading authority on the subject.

In 1969 José was given a scholarship at the Dobie-Paisano Ranch. He was able to spend six months studying and drawing. This was the first time José was able to devote all his time to his art.

After his work at the ranch, José wrote and illustrated a book. It is called *Riders Across the Century: Horsemen of the Spanish Borderlands*. The first drawing in the book is of a soldier in Mexico in 1519. The last picture is of a modern-day *charro*. The book contains 100 pen-and-ink drawings. José also wrote descriptions of each horseman pictured. He even included drawings of a *vaquero* and a Texas Ranger.

After thirty years working for the El Paso Bus Company, José retired. Since that time, he has been able to devote more time to his art. In 1984 he received a great honor. The Cowboy Hall of Fame presented him with the Western Heritage Award.

José has received many honors and has proved him-

José Cisneros

35

self to be a great artist. Yet he constantly strives to improve his drawings. And he feels his new drawings are even better than his older ones.

His work is still being shown in public places, such as the Institute of Texan Cultures in San Antonio. Because of his dedication to art and history, he has made the past come alive for many people. He has also designed emblems and seals, such as the seal for the University of Texas at El Paso. He has designed windows for churches and created wood carvings.

José says that his talent is God-given. Even though he had little art training, he was able to teach himself through careful study and patience.

He is now well-known for his contributions to the world of art. He has realized his dream of becoming a successful artist. José Cisneros is still devoted to achieving excellence in his work.

Patricio Flores
Archbishop of the People

"Listen to me as I tell you about a little boy who toddled behind his father following the harvest north, the young son of a Mexican-American farm laborer. He lived in sheds — sometimes with water and sometimes without. He knew the dull stare of hunger. He saw family-learned prejudice grow in the eyes of his classmates. By the tenth grade, this boy was defeated. And like forty percent of all Mexican-American children, he dropped out of school."

These are the words of Archbishop Patricio (Patrick)

Flores. He is speaking about himself. He overcame his poor background to become the first Mexican-American bishop in the history of the Catholic church. He was also the first Texan to become an archbishop in Texas.

Archbishop Flores has a special place in his heart for the poor. He understands those in prison because he was once in prison for a crime he did not commit. He is quick to defend immigrants since he worked with them as a young boy. He believes that each person is worthwhile and should have a chance to be successful.

The archbishop lives in San Antonio. He is in charge of Catholic churches in thirty-two counties, serving almost 600,000 people. He often travels to different parishes on weekends to hold Mass and to meet the people.

Father Flores was one of nine children in his family. His parents were migrant workers, moving often to pick cotton and other crops. Patricio helped them. When Patricio was eleven, his father began truck farming. Patricio raised turkeys to make extra money at Christmas and at Thanksgiving.

Patricio was a quiet, serious boy. He knew early in life that he wanted to be a priest. He prayed often and studied religion. When he was thirteen years old, he began teaching religion to other children. The nearest church was twenty miles away, too far for them to attend.

Patricio taught himself to type when he was a teenager. When a visiting priest came to his town, Patricio often wrote letters for him. Even at that age, he could express himself well and was skilled at letter writing.

He could also have fun. He and his sister, Mary, entered dance contests around Houston. They wore fancy costumes and often won first place.

But he worked with his parents in the fields too. In the fall, when cotton was ripe, he had to miss school. Because of his absences, he fell behind in his studies.

A nun became interested in him and took him to meet Bishop Byrne in Galveston. The bishop realized that the young man was sincere in his desire to become a priest. He offered to pay his tuition at a Catholic high school in Galveston.

Patrick finally got the chance to realize his dream. He studied hard all week, shining shoes to buy clothes and books. On weekends he worked in his home church in Pearland. He graduated first in his high school class.

He then went to St. Mary's Seminary in La Porte. He studied there for eight years. After graduation, it was customary for a priest to hold his first Mass at his own church. Father Flores returned to Pearland surrounded by his family and friends. It was a happy celebration, with 2,000 people attending.

His first assignment was at a church in the northern part of Houston. The older senior priest did not believe in speaking Spanish, even though most of the church members were Spanish-speaking. Father Flores began having weekend retreats away from the church for the people. He taught them about the Catholic church in their own language. He also believed that religion should be joyful, not solemn. He brought music to these sessions and enjoyed singing himself.

His warm personality and friendliness brought many people back into the church. Its membership grew because of Flores's leadership.

At that time Mexican-Americans were not encouraged to enter the priesthood. Father Flores started an organization called "Los Padres." Its purpose was to encourage Mexican-Americans to become priests.

Some people did not agree with Father Flores's actions, but he was never silent when he felt injustice was present. And he was never afraid to speak for the rights of his people.

Leaders in the Catholic church respected him for his dedication and successes. When there was an opening for an assistant bishop in San Antonio, Flores was asked to fill the vacancy. Archbishop Francis Furey of San Antonio insisted that Flores be assigned as his assistant.

In 1970 Father Flores was made assistant bishop.

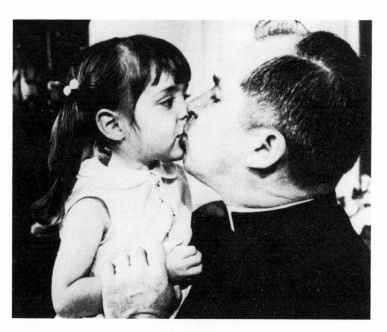

Patrick Flores

The ceremony took place in San Antonio on May 5, a Mexican-American holiday (Cinco de Mayo). People from all over the United States came to see Flores installed as bishop. Mariachi bands played, and children in bright costumes danced at the happy occasion.

Archbishop Flores began at once to take his duties seriously. He helped improve living conditions on the west side of San Antonio. And he encouraged banks to lend money to deserving Mexican-Americans.

The needs of immigrants have always been of much concern to Archbishop Flores. He believes that each person has the right to live and prosper in Texas. He has sponsored classes and leadership training for many Mexican-Americans. Today a large number of these people are leaders in their communities.

Patricio Flores has put the needs of people above all else. He overcame poverty and prejudice to become a priest. He has not forgotten those who must deal with these issues today. As the first Mexican-American bishop in the United States, his life inspires many others to achieve their goals.

Clotilde Garcia

Doctor of the Barrio

It is well past midnight. The telephone rings and Clotilde Garcia is awakened from her sleep. One of her patients is calling to say her baby is coming. Dr. Garcia rushes to the hospital after a long day's work.

After delivering the baby, Dr. Garcia smiles at the newborn child. "My greatest pride is seeing a new being born into this world with the great opportunities for him in the future," she says.

Dr. Cleo, as she is called, has delivered well over 7,000 babies in her thirty years as a doctor. She is sometimes called the "doctor of the barrio." She loves people and is a friend as well as a doctor to her patients.

Garcia wanted to become a doctor when she was a small girl. But it took many years for her dream to come true.

Her parents wanted all seven of their children to become doctors. Six of the seven succeeded. Growing up in a large, loving family was good for Dr. Cleo. She learned to be independent and to think for herself. Competing with her brothers and sisters made her want to achieve.

While attending the University of Texas, she worked at many jobs. She was a bookkeeper, sales clerk, and library assistant. She studied pre-med to prepare for a career in medicine. But she also took education courses that would enable her to teach school.

After graduation, she knew she had to find a job. Her two older brothers were in medical school, and her younger brothers and sisters wanted to go to college.

It was not easy for a Mexican-American woman to find a teaching job in those days. She was finally hired to teach in a two-room ranch school. She earned $800 a year.

During World War II she married a soldier and had a son. When the marriage failed, she had to work to support herself and her child. She also helped her brothers and sisters.

She wondered if she would ever be able to go to medical school. Her brother, Dr. Hector Garcia, encouraged her to apply at the University of Texas.

Few women were accepted into medical school in the 1940s. Women were expected to stay home and raise a family. But Dr. Cleo applied and was accepted. She withdrew $600 from her teacher's retirement to help pay her way.

The school did not encourage Dr. Cleo and the other four women who were accepted. The first year was very difficult. But the five of them realized that they could succeed and did not give up.

Dr. Cleo studied hard and graduated in 1954 near the top of her class. She was one of the first Mexican-American women to enter the medical profession.

She then returned to Corpus Christi to begin her medical practice. She soon learned that she had to teach her patients as well as treat them. Many of them had poor nutrition. Dr. Cleo gained their confidence as she taught them about proper diet and how to care for their bodies.

She is still treating patients and teaching them to develop good health habits. She is especially interested in seeing babies and children develop into healthy adults. Money is not important to Dr. Cleo. Keeping people healthy is her concern.

Dr. Cleo has helped people in other ways besides as a doctor. She joined her brother, Dr. Hector Garcia, in his efforts to see that Mexican-Americans were fairly treated. He organized the American GI Forum after World War II to help veterans receive education, employment, and health benefits.

Dr. Cleo rarely takes a vacation. When she does take a few days off, she studies Texas history. She is especially interested in the role the Mexican people played in the early days when Texas was not even a state.

After studying old records, maps, and books, she wrote and published five books on Mexican history. She is still working on this project. She hopes to create a research center where Mexican-American people can trace their ancestry.

This active woman has worked with twenty-nine different community organizations since 1960. She has given her energy and time to further education, health, employment, and historical projects.

Her list of honors is too long to include. But two

Dr. Clotilde Garcia

stand out as we look at her life. Because of her service to Corpus Christi and to Del Mar College, the college named a building in her honor. It is called the Dr. Clotilde P. Garcia Science and Health Building.

Another great honor came to her in 1984. She was inducted into the first Texas Women's Hall of Fame. She was given this award for her service as a doctor and for her concern for the needs of Mexican-American people. She also has been called a pioneer for women. She was not afraid to pursue a career in a field that men dominated.

Dr. Cleo, doctor of the barrio, continues to be a caring and tireless worker in Corpus Christi.

Hector P. Garcia

Founder of the GI Forum

Hector P. Garcia: doctor, ambassador, civil rights worker, and loyal American. Dr. Garcia has been all these things, working many hours each day helping his fellow man.

As a doctor, he has delivered hundreds of babies and healed the sick. As an ambassador, he has served as the alternate delegate to the United Nations. As a civil rights worker, he has labored tirelessly to make sure that Hispanic and black people receive equal opportunities.

In 1984 President Reagan presented him with the Medal of Freedom. This is the highest honor a president can give a citizen. It is given to those who make outstanding contributions to their country and to their fellow man.

Dr. Garcia remembers hard times when he was young. Although the family was poor, it was a happy, warm family. His parents were important influences in his life. His father was a strict disciplinarian who believed in education. His mother had a deep concern for all people and taught her children to respect others.

As a boy, Hector loved to read, especially history. Two of his heroes are Abraham Lincoln and Benito Juarez. Hector graduated from Mercedes High School, then went to the University of Texas.

His older brother, José Antonio, had gone to medical school and had become a doctor. Hector wanted very much to be a doctor, too. But he did not know if he could afford more education.

The young Hector did not give up easily. He joined the Citizen Military Camp and received a salary during the summer. That helped some, but not enough. His parents wanted all their children to become doctors. They made sacrifices, and his father even sold his life insurance policy to help pay the tuition.

Later, his younger sister, Clotilde, wanted to become a doctor. Hector encouraged her and helped her through medical school.

Dr. Garcia completed his medical internship in Omaha, Nebraska. Then World War II began, and he volunteered to serve his country. His summer military training helped him become a major in the U.S. Army.

He served in the infantry, the Corps of Engineers, and in the Medical Corps. Dr. Garcia earned the Bronze Star with six battle stars for his bravery during the war.

He later returned to Corpus Christi and began his private medical practice. Since he had little money, his office was small. But it was close to the Veterans Administration Center.

He was often asked to examine veterans returning from war. When they were very sick, he wanted to place them in the Naval Air Station Hospital at Corpus

Christi. Most of these veterans were Mexican-Americans. The hospital would not admit them.

Dr. Garcia was very upset about this. He organized a group of veterans to protest this unfair practice. All people who served their country should receive equal rights, he said. Finally, the patients were allowed in the hospital.

Other incidents like this worried Dr. Garcia. He felt that each person should receive equal opportunities.

He organzied the GI Forum to help returning veterans. Dr. Garcia traveled to many cities to begin chapters of this organization. Through his leadership, unfair practices began to change. He fought for equal education, decent housing, and medical care for minorities.

The GI Forum, a veterans' family organization, is active in thirty states. It still serves veterans but reaches their families too. The organization strives for good education for all, awards scholarships, and teaches good citizenship.

Dr. Garcia has received many honors. In 1968 President Lyndon Johnson appointed him U.S. civil rights commissioner. Presidents Kennedy and Carter have called on him to lend his wisdom and leadership. And, of course, the Medal of Freedom award given by President Reagan is as high an honor as any citizen can receive.

Although he has a busy medical practice in Corpus Christi, Dr. Garcia stays involved with his community and his people. In 1986 he received an award, "Honor al Merito," in Mexico City.

Another honor came to him in 1985. A teaching position was created in his name at Yale University in Connecticut. Also during that year, the city of Corpus Christi named a park after him, the Hector P. Garcia Park.

He is married to the former Wanda Fusillo and they have three adult children. Dr. Garcia has dedicated his life to help all people, regardless of race or color, receive equal opportunities. He still feels that much needs to be done. He hopes that more Mexican-Americans will grad-

Dr. Hector P. Garcia

uate from high school and go to college. He wants them to have better jobs and higher incomes.

Dr. Garcia is still giving his time and energy to bring about progress.

Reynaldo Garza

United States Federal Judge

"What do you want to be when you grow up?" Reynaldo's brother asked him.

"A lawyer," the third-grader replied.

Most children change their minds many times before they choose their lifework. But Reynaldo never changed his mind about becoming a lawyer.

He had two older brothers who were starting college when he was starting elementary school. "You must speak English a great deal, so that you can understand your teacher," they told him.

Reynaldo today feels that this was good advice. He did so well in the first grade that he skipped the second. He liked to go to bed early and rise early. There was no television in those days, and people had to use earphones to listen to the radio. Since Reynaldo was one of eight children, he rarely got the chance to listen.

He was an active boy and enjoyed playing with his neighborhood friends in Brownsville. He especially liked to play baseball and marbles.

Reynaldo was well-liked by his classmates. When he was in the fifth grade, they elected him president of the class. They continued to choose him as president during junior and senior high school.

Reynaldo Garza

His role as a leader helped him to become the first Mexican-American federal judge. He has been successful as a judge since 1961.

In high school, Reynaldo acted in plays and took part in all activities. As a senior, he was chosen to be editor of the yearbook.

Money was scarce about the time he graduated from high school. The country was in a depression, and Reynaldo stayed at home and attended a junior college for two years.

He then entered the University of Texas at Austin. He earned two degrees at the university, a B.A. degree and a law degree.

Judge Garza returned to Brownsville and practiced law for four years. Because the U.S. was in World War II, he enlisted in the air force. He was an aerial gunner and taught others that skill.

After three years in the air force, Judge Garza was discharged and reestablished his law practice in Brownsville. During this time he served on the Brownsville School Board and on the city council.

In 1961 President John Kennedy appointed him United States district judge for the Southern District of Texas. It was the first time a Mexican-American had received such an honor.

As a federal judge, Judge Garza has always tried to be fair to all people. He takes his responsibilities seriously and shows wisdom in the courtroom.

In 1970 he spoke out for black and Mexican-American longshoremen. At that time, unions were segregated. There was a union for white men, and unions for non-whites.

Some of the men felt that minorities were not getting fair treatment. Unions gave more jobs to the white men. Judge Garza ruled that this was an unfair practice. Since that time, minorities have been given equal treatment.

Judge Garza also has defended students. He ruled

that they have the right to disagree with administrations, as long as they do so in a peaceful manner.

Although he has many duties, he has always felt he should help his community. He has been active in the Rotary Club, the United Fund, and in other organizations in Brownsville.

He has also been an active member of the Catholic church. He has been especially interested in the men's service group, Knights of Columbus. Because of his service to this group, the Pope awarded him a medal.

Judge Garza shows his interest in young people in many ways. He is a past member of the board of governors of St. Mary's University and is a trustee of the law school. He has been a member of the executive board of the Boy Scouts of America in the Rio Grande area.

Judge Garza is married and is the father of five children. He was promoted to appeals judge in the District of New Orleans. He maintains his home in Brownsville, but presides over the court in New Orleans when he is needed.

Henry B. Gonzalez

United States Congressman

Henry B. Gonzalez grew up on the west side of San Antonio. He did not speak English until he started to school. He loved to read and visited the library often to borrow books. As a boy, he liked to read westerns. Later, he became interested in history books.

Henry B., as he is called, also liked math and science. He planned to have a career in engineering. But his ambitions changed when he became interested in law and politics.

He was the first Mexican-American elected to the Texas Senate. He was also the first to be elected to the United States Congress. He has served government for more than thirty years.

It was natural that Henry B. would enter politics. His father had been the mayor of a city in Mexico. Politics was a tradition in the Gonzalez family.

Henry B. worked himself through San Antonio Junior College and attended the University of Texas at Austin. His interest in law caused him to enroll at St. Mary's Law School in San Antonio. He received two degrees from the school. He worked part-time in the law library for $30 a month to help pay his expenses.

After graduation, Henry B. became a juvenile probation officer. He tried to help young people who were in trouble with the law. He walked the back streets and alleys of San Antonio. He tried to understand the problems of teenagers. His experience working with the poor and those in trouble greatly influenced him. Henry B. never forgot the poverty he saw and has never stopped trying to help the poor.

Henry B. became chief probation officer for the county. He was the first Mexican-American to hold this position.

Henry B.'s ancestors were early Spanish settlers in Mexico. His great-grandfather fought in the Mexican Revolution. The family had to leave Mexico because of the revolution. They moved to Laredo first and later to San Antonio.

His father became the manager of a Spanish-language newspaper, *La Prensa*. As a boy, Henry B. visited the newspaper office often. He met community leaders and listened to them talk about government. For a while he was a translator for the newspaper.

After serving as chief probation officer, he decided

Henry B. Gonzalez

he wanted to be more active in government. In 1950 he ran for the San Antonio City Council and won.

Henry B. Gonzalez has never been afraid to speak his mind. As soon as he became councilman, he tried to correct unfairness in the city. At that time in San Antonio, and in other places, some people could not swim in city pools. Henry B. did not think this was right. He made sure that all people, regardless of race, could use city pools and buildings.

Three years later, Henry B. was elected state senator. He helped pass laws to tear down slums and replace them with proper housing. He also fought to see that all people could go to public restaurants. At that time, only whites were allowed.

Some people did not agree with the senator from San Antonio. They wanted to keep the races separate. Senator Gonzalez once talked for thirty-six hours to keep a segregation law from passing. He felt that people should be free to live and work wherever they pleased.

Henry B. has not been popular with everyone. But popularity is not important to him. Bringing about justice for all people is more important.

In 1961 he was elected a U.S. congressman from San Antonio. He left the state capital in Austin and headed for Washington, D.C. One of his first concerns was to make sure that all people had the right to vote. He did not believe that anyone should have to pay a tax to vote. He also worked hard to improve housing in America. He wanted to replace slums with decent places to live.

Henry B. has served on the Banking Committee for many years in the nation's capital. He has helped many small businesses and kept them from going bankrupt.

In 1968 Henry B. helped bring a world's fair to San Antonio. He was able to get cooperation from nations all over the world to do this. Hemisfair '68 was a big success and brought many visitors to San Antonio. Today San Antonio is a leading convention center, largely because of Henry B.'s efforts.

This U.S. congressman has also made it possible for his home city of San Antonio to receive millions of dollars from the national government. The money has been used for housing, hospitals, and military bases. He has worked hard for his city, his state, and his country.

Recently, Henry B. spoke against nuclear power plants. He desires world peace and feels he must speak against nuclear power to ensure such peace.

Henry B. Gonzalez is married and has eight children. He is a tall, muscular man who is easily recognized by everyone. He often dresses like a southern gentleman.

He has been a pioneer as a Mexican-American in government service. His courage and leadership have given others hope and encouragement. He was the first Mexican-American in Texas to become a state senator and a United States congressman.

Congressman Gonzalez is proud that he has always represented all people, not just those of his race. He feels it is his duty to speak for people and their rights.

As he said, "If I have achieved anything in Texas politics, it is to have established the idea that a minority politician can represent the whole community."

Ninfa Rodriguez Laurenzo

Businesswoman

Ninfa Laurenzo learned about the business world when she was a teenager. Her brother-in-law owned several small grocery stores. When he and his wife went on vacation, Ninfa was left to manage the stores.

As a teenager, she loved the work and learned a

great deal. She decided she would like to own a business of her own someday. She was only a teenager, but she had a dream. Today Ninfa's restaurants are worth millions of dollars in Houston.

Ninfa was born in Harlingen, Texas. Since she was the youngest of twelve children, she learned early in life to be independent. After she grew up, she visited her sister in Rhode Island. There she met Tommy Laurenzo. They fell in love and were married.

The young couple decided that Houston would be a good place to live and to work. They moved to the city and together began the Rio Grande Food Products Company. They manufactured pizza dough and tortillas. This seemed a natural thing to do, with Tommy being Italian and Ninfa being a Mexican-American.

They built a home next to the factory and also started a family of five children. As each child became old enough, he or she worked in the business. With hard work the business became successful.

Ninfa and Tommy dreamed of someday having a restaurant. Then suddenly, in 1969, Tommy died. Ninfa had five children to support and knew she had to continue the business. But there were money problems. To earn more money, Ninfa decided to open a small restaurant in part of the factory.

She mortgaged her house and borrowed $5,000 from a friend. She took a small area of the factory and converted it into a ten-table Mexican restaurant. At first she used her own pots, pans, even plates and silverware.

A week after the little restaurant opened, a fire broke out. Ninfa and her children were a united team as they worked to restore the restaurant. They were able to reopen it only a week later.

The businessmen who stopped there for lunch were surprised to find such good food. Ninfa was not serving the same foods as most Mexican restaurants did. She cooked many of the foods that were served in Mexico, such as flautas and sopapillas. Then she added a recipe of

Ninfa Laurenzo

her own and called it "Tacos al Carbon." This dish has since made her famous.

Soon an evening crowd began coming to the restaurant inside the factory. People had to wait a long time just to get a table. Ninfa knew what she had to do. She took another part of the factory and added twenty-four tables. When this proved too small, she borrowed money and doubled the size of the restaurant.

Ninfa and her children were joyful over the success. When an opportunity came to open a second Ninfa's, she wondered if she should take the risk. She remembers, "Some of us were afraid we'd lose everything. I thought, 'I know how to be poor. What was the difference?' "

The family decided to take the chance. They opened a second Ninfa's, then a third. Today there are ten restaurants in the Houston area, all of them successful. The Laurenzo family has also added an Italian and a seafood restaurant.

Although Ninfa is very busy with many duties, she still finds time to give to her city and community. She has been active in many organizations and has served as honorary chairman of the American Cancer Society in Houston. She has also been active in Big Brothers and Sisters, an organization which helps children.

Ninfa serves on the advisory board of Texas A&I University in Kingsville. She is a popular speaker at different events in Texas. She has taken a special interest in addressing women who want to achieve in business.

Many honors have come her way. In 1981 and 1983 the National Hispanic Chamber of Commerce named her "Business Woman of the Year." The Texas Restaurant Association chose her as the outstanding woman in the restaurant business. She has appeared on local and national television.

Ninfa is a woman who refuses to let disappointment discourage her. She has never been afraid of hard work. Her optimistic attitude has helped her achieve her goals.

Several years ago, a musical play was written about her life and was presented in Houston.

Ninfa Laurenzo built a million-dollar business in only ten years. She is proud of her restaurants and proud of the food that is served there. She is respected in Texas as an outstanding citizen and a very successful business-woman.

Lydia Mendoza

Meadowlark of the Border

Lydia Mendoza is known as "La Alondra de la Fron-tera," the meadowlark of the border. Since she was four years old, Lydia has loved music. Now in her seventies, Lydia still enjoys singing and playing her guitar for others.

All the members of her family were musical, but Lydia is the only one who has pursued a musical career. This pioneer in Mexican-American music has brought joy to countless people over a sixty-year period.

She was the first Texan to receive the National Heritage Award from the National Endowment for the Arts. She was chosen to receive this award because of her contributions to music. She developed "Musica Nortena," a style of music that combines the German folk accordion style with the Mexican twelve-string guitar.

Lydia was born in Houston but also lived in Mexico and in other states. Her father was a mechanic for the railroad and worked on both sides of the border. He frequently took his family with him. He did not believe that girls needed educations. Lydia's mother taught the children at home and was a good teacher. By the time the children were five years old, they could read.

Both Lydia's father and mother played the guitar. With her natural talent, Lydia started playing it, too, when she was seven years old.

There was no radio or television when Lydia was a child. She loved to sing and wanted to learn the words of songs. She collected gum wrappers that had the words of songs written inside. She learned songs like "El Rancho Grande" this way.

When Lydia was a child, she lived for a while in Monterrey, Mexico. On Saturday nights a group of musicians would gather at the corner grocery store to play and sing. Lydia loved to listen to them, and soon she was performing too.

Since the family was musical, they began performing together. Her mother played the guitar; her father played the tambourine; her sister played the triangle; and Lydia played the mandolin. At age twelve, Lydia learned to play the violin. But the guitar eventually became her favorite.

The family became migrant musicians, traveling all over the country, wherever the migrant workers could be found. They entertained the working people and brought joy to their lives. The group was so successful that Lydia's father quit his job at the railroad so the family could travel and perform.

They finally returned to San Antonio and began making records. A Spanish radio announcer recognized Lydia's talent when she was seventeen years old. She entered an amateur contest and won first place. After this, she began singing professionally on the radio, earning $3.50 a week.

Lydia's trademark was her twelve-string guitar, which she strung herself. She sang the songs she learned as a child, but her favorite was, and is, the *corrido*, the ballad, a song that comes from the heart.

For many years the family traveled, entertaining

Lydia Mendoza
— Houston Public Library

Mexican-Americans from Texas to California. Lydia and her mother made the colorful costumes the family wore. She still likes to sew and make her own Mexican-type dresses. The family continued to perform until Lydia's mother died.

Lydia Mendoza has achieved national and international fame. She has sung at the White House and at the Library of Congress in Washington, D.C.

The day before her seventy-first birthday, she gave a concert at the Museum of Fine Arts in Houston. The audience loved her music and applauded her skillful guitar playing and her still clear, strong voice.

"I feel a lot of happiness through music. The songs I sing and the public who still comes to hear me — those are my big loves," she says.

"I'll probably die with a guitar in my hands," she told a close friend.

Irma Rangel

State Legislator

Irma Rangel has always been interested in people. When she was a child, her parents taught her to help others. She decided she could do this best by becoming a lawmaker.

Rangel is the first Mexican-American woman to become a state legislator. She has served Texas since 1977.

She was born in Kingsville and attended school there. Her parents had been field workers. But by hard work, they have become owners of successful businesses. They are also leaders in their community.

The Rangels wanted Irma to study business in college. But when she attended Texas A&I University, she knew she wanted to be a teacher.

She began teaching elementary school in the towns of Alice and Robstown. Then the spirit of adventure led her to Caracas, Venezuela. She taught the children of people who were employed by oil companies. Later, she became principal of the school.

After fourteen years as an educator, Irma decided to leave the field of teaching. It was time to pursue her dream of becoming a lawyer. She had thought about this since she was a teenager. An older lawyer had shown her that the rights of people could be protected by law.

Irma felt that she could help people more by becoming a lawyer. She attended St. Mary's Law School in San Antonio and graduated in 1969. Her first job was as a law clerk for Judge Adrian Spears. She then became the assistant district attorney in Corpus Christi.

In that position she learned much about the problems of people. She saw the results of poverty and juvenile delinquency. She never forgot these problems when she became a state legislator.

Next, she worked for a law firm in Corpus Christi. After gaining experience there, she returned to her hometown of Kingsville and opened her own law firm.

At that time she decided to enter politics. She ran for Democratic county chairperson and won. She gives credit to her family and friends for helping her win the election.

Once when she was attending a meeting in Austin, she realized there were no Mexican-American women in the state government. She decided to be a pioneer and try for a leadership role in Texas.

Rangel had little money to spend in a campaign, but this did not stop her. She walked from house to house and talked to people, mostly women, about her ideas. The people liked what she said and supported her. Even though many of them were poor migrant workers, they donated money to her campaign for legislator.

Irma Rangel

When election day came, Irma won. She says that she could not have succeeded without the help of the people who believed in her.

As a new legislator, Irma Rangel took a strong stand to pass a law that would help women with children. She introduced a bill to help them get education and employment. She felt that if people had a helping hand, they could work and support themselves.

Rangel has tried to help the women of Texas. She has also been active in issues that would benefit Mexican-Americans.

Education and employment have always been high on her list as a lawmaker. She believes that education is the key to success. She has also tried to bring about fair voting practices and supported farm workers.

She is a firm believer in a strong family life. Her own family is very important to her. Because of her parents' influence, she has given her life to public service.

"It is important to maintain respect and love for parents," she says.

Her life is very busy. She spends part of her time as a lawmaker at the state capital. She also continues to work at her own law practice in Kingsville.

"Work hard — it will bring its own rewards," she says.

Besides her work as lawmaker and as lawyer, Irma Rangel gives time to her community. She has been active in many organizations both in Corpus Christi and in Kingsville.

Irma is a pioneer as a Mexican-American woman in public service. But she feels others will follow her in the future. She would like to see more Mexican-American women take part in the business world and in politics.

Irma Rangel has earned the respect of other lawmakers since she was elected. She has helped the people of Texas in many ways by her dedicated service.

Tomás Rivera
Poet, Scholar, Musician

When Tomás Rivera was a small boy, he and his family traveled, picking fruits and vegetables. They rode in the back of a truck to Utah, Minnesota, Michigan, and other states.

Although his home was in Crystal City, Texas, Tomás had to leave when his family found work. He attended school about six months out of the year, from November to April. Tomás worked at this job until he was twenty years old. He wrote a book about his experiences many years later.

Tomás knew how it felt to pick beets or spinach all day. He knew the loneliness of being in a strange place. And he knew how it was to be poor and to wear old clothes.

He couldn't speak English when he first started to school. It took five years before he was able to speak, read, and write the language. When he finished high school in Crystal City, he was very proud. But he wanted to learn more.

Although his parents had little education, they encouraged Tomás. He wanted to go to college, but he knew he would have to work hard and to make it on his own. Making the decision to begin college was the turning point in his life.

He worked and attended Southwest Junior College for two years. He liked to learn and wanted more educa-

66

Tomás Rivera
— Tomás Rivera Archive, University
of California, Riverside

tion. He enrolled at Southwest Texas State University and earned his bachelor's degree.

Tomás began his career as a teacher. He taught English in San Antonio and in Crystal City for several years. He then returned to Southwest Texas to work on his master's degree. To help pay his tuition, he taught English, Spanish, and French.

After this, he went to the University of Oklahoma to study for his doctoral degree. He often gave talks about migrant workers there. He also became director of the language laboratory at the school. Because of his training, he became a college professor. He taught at Sam Houston State University and at the University of Texas at San Antonio.

While he was teaching, he also wrote stories and poetry. He published a book, *y no se lo trago la tierra (The Earth Did Not Swallow)*. This book contains fourteen stories about migrant workers. Rivera could remember almost every detail of his life when he picked fruits and vegetables. He could recall the pain and suffering of those who worked so hard. He also remembered their courage and spirit.

Some of his stories are about a boy growing up. Others are told by an old man. He could tell a good story and make people laugh and cry.

Quinta Sol Publications awarded him their first National Literary Award in 1970 for this book. It is read by scholars and students today as the best book written about migrant workers.

Rivera continued to write, but his career took a different turn. He was offered the job of chancellor at the University of California, Riverside. He accepted the position and became the first Mexican-American to supervise the school. He was also the youngest chancellor ever appointed.

Rivera helped many people, regardless of race, to get an education. He had so many duties, though, that he had little time for his writing. He began another book, but he died in 1984 before it was finished.

His early death was a loss to many people. He had set an example as a person who worked hard to achieve his goals. He was proud of being a Mexican-American and loved the history and culture of the Mexican people.

Tomás Rivera was a successful teacher and university leader. His writings, especially his book, were important contributions to literature. He began as a poor migrant worker who couldn't speak English. But he died a successful leader and writer who won't be forgotten.

Lee Trevino
Super Golfer

Lee Trevino, champion golfer, didn't see a golf ball until he was almost eight years old. The first seven years of his life were spent in the country with his mother and grandfather. Lee enjoyed fishing and hunting as a child.

His grandfather was a tenant farmer. By the time Lee was five years old, he was working in the fields. He planted onions and picked cotton to help his grandfather.

Then, when Lee was seven, the family moved to Dallas. They lived only 100 yards from the golf course of the Dallas Athletic Club. Lee noticed that the men were hitting small balls with metal rods. He didn't know what they were doing or what the game was all about.

Since he was curious, Lee watched the men at their sport. He wandered about the golf course and picked up balls for the men. Since he was a friendly boy, the men liked him. They soon began paying him to carry their golf bags for them. Lee was glad to have the job, since his grandfather worked hard but did not earn much money.

Sometimes when the caddies finished working for the golfers, they played each other behind the clubhouse. Lee was a natural with a golf club and usually beat the other caddies.

He was also good at other sports, including baseball and football. He is sorry now that he didn't apply himself in school. He dropped out before finishing high school and has always felt he had to try harder than anyone else in everything he did.

When Lee was seventeen years old, he decided to join the Marines. He left on December 19, just before Christmas. Lee said Christmas was not a big celebration at his house, since there was never enough money to buy presents.

Money was scarce when he was a child. He doesn't remember having candy. In 1968, after winning the U.S. Open Tournament, he helped give a party for underprivileged children and bought $1,200 worth of candy for them.

When he was in the Marines, Lee trained as a machine gunner but never saw combat duty. He spent time in Japan and in Okinawa, then returned to the United States in 1957. Since he liked the Marines, he reenlisted for three more years.

He was fortunate enough to be assigned to Special Services and thus became involved in athletics. He managed equipment and helped transport football teams to games. In his spare time he played golf. He became so skilled in the game that he qualified for the golf team. That team won the Okinawa Club Championship.

In 1960 Lee was discharged from the Marines. He considers his experience in the service rewarding and one that gave him self-discipline. He always sent half of his monthly pay home to his mother and grandfather.

After his experience as a Marine, he started working for a golf course. He did many jobs, such as mending

Lee Trevino

clubs and cutting weeds. At night, after his work was finished, he practiced golf. A year later, he was considered a professional golfer.

His game continued to improve and in 1966 he won fifty-fourth place in the U.S. Open. He had the thrill of winning $600 for his victory. Only one year later, he entered the U.S. Open again and beat Jack Nicklaus, expert golfer. This achievement won him $6,000, a huge sum to him at that time. A short time later, he bought a new house for his mother and grandfather.

Lee was on his way to becoming one of the best golfers in the United States. In 1973 he tied for second place in the Danny Thomas-Memphis Classic and earned the enormous sum of $1 million.

Lee was an entertainer on the golf course as well as a talented golfer. He joked and always had something funny to say. He probably developed this trait from his mother. Although her life was never easy, she had a sense of humor and a happy nature. One of Lee's greatest satisfactions was knowing his grandfather lived long enough to see his grandson become successful.

Although Lee laughs and jokes a lot on the golf course, off the course he is a very private person. He needs time to himself and doesn't mind being alone.

One of his greatest achievements came in 1974, when he won first place in the Professional Golfers Association Tournament. Playing against the greatest pro golfers, he won by beating Jack Nicklaus. That same year he also beat Gary Player in the World Series of Golf. His prize was $50,000.

Lee has won many more tournaments, too many to mention. He has traveled all over the world and has been invited to the White House by four presidents: Nixon, Ford, Carter, and Reagan.

At one point in his career he developed a serious back problem and had to have spinal surgery. Always a fighter, Lee was back on the golf course in only eighteen months. He entered the Canadian Open Tournament and won first place. Because of this, the Golf Writers of America voted to give him the Ben Hogan Award. This is given to a player who overcomes a serious handicap.

Perhaps his biggest honor came when he was received into the World Golf Hall of Fame in 1981. He considers this the high point in his life, one that he will never forget.

Lee has never let physical problems or age keep him from trying his best. In 1984, at the age of forty-four, he again proved he was golf's best player by winning the Professional Golfers Association Tournament. He did this with a record-shattering performance on the golf course.

There have been many great golfers, but Lee Trevino remains one of America's favorites.

Emma Tenayuca

Champion of the People

Emma Tenayuca fought for people's rights. She had rocks thrown at her and was even put in jail because of her courage.

She was in her early twenties when she became aware of injustice. Mexican-Americans in San Antonio were not being paid fair salaries. This made her angry and made her risk her life to bring about change.

In the 1930s the pecan industry was the main business in San Antonio. In fact, the city was the pecan capital of the world. The trees were grown in Texas and the pecans shipped to San Antonio. There the nuts were cracked, shelled, and shipped all over the country.

Most of the people who cracked and shelled pecans were Mexican-Americans. In 1938 they were paid about six cents per pound for their work. A sheller might work seventy-five hours a week and earn only $2.73.

Because of the low salaries, the people could not afford decent places to live. Many had no running water, plumbing, or electricity. These unsanitary conditions caused disease and sometimes death.

Emma became angry at this injustice. She talked with the pecan workers. She advised them to speak out for their rights. The people did ask for a raise, but they were turned down. In fact, their pay was cut.

The people were hungry and sick, but they tried to work. Emma advised them to stop working and go on strike. Perhaps the pecan companies would see how much they needed the workers and would raise their pay.

About 10,000 people went on strike. Emma and many others were arrested by the police. She was put in jail, but she was not afraid. She knew she was right in speaking out for unfairness.

The strike was successful. The pecan workers were given pay raises and other benefits. Within a short time, though, the companies began using machines to do the work. But Emma did not regret her actions. She felt that the workers had proven to everyone that they had rights and would not be abused.

Emma also worked with garment workers who earned little money and had to work under poor conditions. She helped cement and laundry workers to receive fair treatment and wages during the 1940s.

Emma's childhood seems to have caused her to be sensitive to the needs of people. She was raised by her grandparents, who were honest, religious people. She remembers that they accepted every person, regardless of race or color. Through her grandparents, she realized that all people deserve to have lives of dignity and justice.

She remembers that her uncles and her grandfather

Emma Tenayuca
— Institute of Texan Cultures,
San Antonio

always discussed politics. They talked of events in San Antonio and always voted in elections. Emma was interested in what they said.

She was taken to the plaza as a child and heard many speeches. She listened as others spoke of injustices in the city. When she was very young, she became interested in people and the world around her.

Emma is part Indian and part Spanish. Her ancestors were living in Texas before European settlers came. In high school Emma was a good student. She read many books and discussed them with her friends. She was aware of important happenings in the United States.

In the late 1940s, Emma went to California and completed college. She graduated from the University of San Francisco. In the 1960s she returned to San Antonio and taught school for many years. She eventually retired and remained in San Antonio.

The older people in that city remember Emma's bravery during the famous pecan strike in 1938. She is considered a heroine to many. It was Emma Tenayuca who gave the workers courage to speak for themselves.

The action they took put an end to persecution of Mexican-Americans in the city. It made businesses and industry realize that every human being has rights and should not be treated unfairly.

Emma continues working in her district, campaigning for candidates she feels will represent the people. She is especially interested in seeing women take more leadership roles in government.

"Women can make a difference," she says, with a twinkle in her brown eyes.

Emma Tenayuca certainly made a difference to many people during the Depression years.

Felix and Janie Tijerina

Friends of the Children

When Felix Tijerina was a boy, he worked side by side with his parents, picking cotton and other crops. He did not have a chance to go to school.

He traveled the dusty roads of Texas, doing farm chores with other migrant workers. When Felix was ten, his father died. The boy had to help support his mother and three sisters. He worked long hours in the cotton fields for four years. Then, at the age of fourteen, he moved to Houston.

Felix got a job as a busboy in a restaurant, earning $9 per week. But he could speak no English. His boss told him, "Felix, if you want to get ahead, learn to speak English."

So Felix began learning English by reading catsup bottles and the menu. He also took a six-month course in a public night school.

About ten years later, when he was twenty-three, Felix opened his own restaurant. Because the Depression had begun, and people had no money to eat out, the restaurant closed.

Felix did not give up, however. He later opened restaurants in Houston and in Beaumont. The Felix Mexican Restaurants are still popular today, after more than fifty years. Mrs. Janie Tijerina, Felix's widow, owns and manages them.

Mr. Felix, as he was then called, was not content just to earn money. He knew how lost he had felt as a young boy who did not know English. And he knew that many Mexican-American children entered school without speaking English. He felt that was the reason many failed or dropped out of school.

He wanted to help these children. He had heard of a teacher, Mrs. Elizabeth Burrus, who was very successful with Mexican-American children. He decided to visit her and learn the key to her success.

Mrs. Burrus told him that she began by teaching children the basic words they needed in first grade. She showed him a list of 400 English words that were important for children starting school.

Mr. Felix had the vocabulary words printed in booklet form. Using his own money, he started two free summer schools for children about to enter school. These schools were in Ganado and Edna, Texas. He called them "Little Schools of the 400" because of the 400-word list.

He hired teachers and even taught classes himself. Forty-two children attended these schools for six weeks. When the children finished the first grade, every one of them passed. The year before, more than half had failed.

These classes were only the beginning. The following year, Mr. Felix opened seven more schools in Houston. He knew many more were needed. He asked the Texas legislature for help in paying for them. He was overjoyed when the state agreed to spend money for the Little Schools.

He knew that parents would have to be convinced that their children needed these classes. The news was broadcast in Spanish over thirty-eight radio stations. Television channels showed films of the program. Newspapers and even Boy Scouts spread the word.

When the Little Schools opened their doors, more than 15,000 children attended. Specially trained teachers used films, pictures, and records to teach the 400 English words to the students.

Today there are classes in public schools for students who do not speak English. But there were no classes during the 1950s. Mr. Felix was a pioneer in starting English classes for Spanish- speaking children.

Why did this successful businessman use his own time and money to develop these programs? Before his

Felix Tijerina

Janie Tijerina

— Houston Public Library

death, he said, "A man does not wish just to take from his community. He must give, as well."

Mr. Felix never stopped giving his time and money to others. He helped many young people go to college. He was director of the Rotary Club, a service organization. He helped hospitals, youth groups, and the Houston Opera.

He was also elected president of LULAC (League of Latin American Citizens), a national organization. With the help of this group, the Little Schools spread to New Jersey, New York, New Mexico, and California.

Mr. Felix bought a set of law books in order to study and understand legal matters. He was always learning. Even though he was a successful businessman and leader in his community, his main interest was in education. He had to struggle alone in order to learn. He wanted to make it easier for young people.

He often made speeches and spoke with educators in other states about the Little Schools. They respected and admired him.

Mr. Felix came a long way from the day he entered that restaurant in Houston. He never forgot having to learn his first English from the label on a catsup bottle. And Mr. Felix never forgot to help others.

Janie Tijerina took over when her husband died. She continues to manage three restaurants and to contribute to her community.

The energetic Mrs. Felix, as she is called, begins her day early in the morning. She visits her restaurants, inspects the kitchens, and makes sure the restaurants are properly managed. Often she must dash to committee meetings or interviews. Her day does not end until 7:00 in the evening.

Every Tuesday morning she is at her original restaurant to buy the food from salesmen. She wants to make sure only the best quality is used in the restaurant.

"I want my customers to come back again," she says. And many of her customers have been eating at Felix

Mexican Restaurant for forty years. She knows many of them by name.

Mrs. Felix became the first woman in Houston to be admitted to the Rotary Club. She has also been on the board of directors of the Salvation Army, March of Dimes, and Boys Club.

She likes young people and believes they are the future of our country. She has taken a personal interest in many who have just arrived in the United States and has helped them learn English.

Mrs. Felix was behind her husband's efforts in starting the Little Schools. She says that some schools are still using the same 400-word method to teach first-graders English.

Bibliography

Andrea Castanon Ramirez Candalaria
Callihan, Dr. D. Jeanne, and Samuel Nesmith. *Our Mexican Ances-tors.* San Antonio: Institute of Texan Cultures, 1981 (107–110).
Houston Press, March 2, 1931.
San Antonio Light, February 19, 1899.
Texas Women's Hall of Fame, 1986. Texas Woman's University, Den-ton, Texas.

Lorenzo de Zavala
Allen, Edward. *Heroes of Texas.* New York: Julian Messner, 1970 (69–75).
Fehrenbach, T. R. *Lone Star.* New York: American Legacy Press, 1983 (222–223).
Mexican Texans. San Antonio: Institute of Texan Cultures, 1971.
Venable, Faye. *North Toward the Rio Grande.* Austin: Eakin Press, 1985.

Erasmo and Juan Seguin
Kerr, Rita. *Juan Seguin.* Austin: Eakin Press, 1985.
Mexican Texans. San Antonio: Institute of Texan Cultures, 1971.
Ramsdell, Charles. "Casa Blanca." *San Antonio Express,* May 21, 1948.
"Remains of Native San Antonian." *San Antonio Express,* September 17, 1974.
Seguin, Juan. Personal memoirs. Daughters of Republic of Texas Li-brary.

The Gregorio Esparza Family
Callihan, Dr. D. Jeanne, and Samuel Nesmith. *Our Mexican Ances-tors.* San Antonio: Institute of Texan Cultures, 1981 (97–106).
Malkowski, Karen. "Boy Hovers in Carnage, Tells Story to Descen-dants." *San Antonio Express News,* March 2, 1986. (Recount of Enrique Esparza's story from *Daily Express,* 1907.)
Mexican Texans. San Antonio: Institute of Texan Cultures, 1971.

83

José Antonio Navarro

Dawson, Joseph Martin. *José Antonio Navarro: Co-Creator of Texas.* Waco: Baylor University Press, 1969.

José Antonio Navarro, written by an old Texan, 1876. Preface by Mary Bell Hart.

Mexican Texans. San Antonio: Institute of Texan Cultures, 1971.

Roy Benavidez

Allsup, Dan. "The Private War of Roy Benavidez." *Houston Post,* January 4, 1987.

Benavidez, Roy, and Oscar Griffin. *The Three Wars of Roy Benavidez.* San Antonio: Corona Publishing.

Hammond, Ken. "Hero." *Houston Chronicle–Texas Magazine,* January 31, 1982.

The Cavazos Family

Cochran, Mike. "Rancher's Sons Amass Triumphs Fit For a King." *Austin American-Statesman,* March 14, 1982.

Danini, Carmina. "Texas Tech Scholarship Cites Tomasa Cavazos." [Laredo] *Morning Times,* November 8, 1987.

"Kingsville Honors Distinguished Son." *Kingsville Record,* January 18, 1984.

Lea, Tom. *The King Ranch.* Boston: Little Brown, 1957.

Meier, Matt S. *Mexican American Biographies.* New York: Greenwood Press.

Who's Who in America, 1982–83. Marquis Who's Who, Chicago.

Henry Cisneros

Burka, Paul. "Henry B. and Henry C." *Texas Monthly,* February 1986.

Diehl, Kemper, and Jan Jarboe. *Henry Cisneros.* San Antonio: Corona Publishing Co., 1985.

Lemann, Nicholas. "First Hispanic." *Esquire,* December 1984.

José Cisneros

Cisneros, José, with biography by John O. West. *Riders Across the Centuries.* El Paso: Texas Western Press.

Davis, Mary Margaret. "El Pasoan's Drawings Are All the Rage in San Antonio." *El Paso Times,* March 13, 1988.

Havel, Odette. "A Horseman's Horseman." *El Paso Times,* January 6, 1985.

Hertzog, J. Carl. "Tribute to José Cisneros." Publisher unknown.

Salazar, Veronica. "Cisneros Sketches Way to Top." *San Antonio Express News,* November 3, 1974.

Sammons, Marc. "The Riders of the Border Are His Legacy." *Santa Fe Reporter,* November 21, 1982.

Walker, Dale. "Prose, Drawings Reflect Character of José Cisneros." *El Paso Times,* December 2, 1984.

Patricio Flores
Davidson, John. "A Simple Man." *Texas Monthly,* July 1987.
Phelon, Craig. "Archbishop Patrick Flores." *San Antonio Express News,* May 2, 1982.
Sandoval, Moises. "Minister to His People." *Modern Ministries,* March 1982.

Clotilde Garcia
Hinojosa, Aida. "Clotilde P. Garcia — Doctor of the Barrio." Unpublished.
Salazar, Veronica. "Dedication Rewarded." *San Antonio Light Express.*
Texas Women's Hall of Fame. "Dr. Clotilde Garcia." Texas Woman's University, Denton. 1984.
Letter from Dr. Clotilde P. Garcia to Sammye Munson.

Hector P. Garcia
Chacon, Jose Andres, and Felix Padilla. "Dr. Hector P. Garcia." *San Antonio Express News,* October 3, 1971.
Moore, John Paul. "A Man for Mexican Americans." *Texas Star,* March 25, 1973.
Letter from Dr. Hector Garcia to Sammye Munson.

Reynaldo Garza
Garza, Reynaldo, biography. Institute of Texan Cultures.
Letter from Reynaldo Garza to Sammye Munson.
Mexican Texans. San Antonio: Institute of Texan Cultures, 1971.

Henry B. Gonzalez
"Congressional Voice For the Poor." *America,* March 8, 1986.
Burka, Paul. "Henry B. and Henry C." *Texas Monthly,* February 1986.
Nash, Deanna, ed. "Congressman Gonzalez and Mayo." Citizens Look at Congress.
National Catholic Reporter, February 25, 1983.
"Profile of a Public Man." *Nuestro,* March 7, 1983.
Letter from Henry B. Gonzalez to Sammye Munson.

Ninfa Rodriguez Laurenzo
Freeman, Diane. "Ninfa's Strategy: New Foods, Cities." *Houston Post,* June 5, 1981.
Lasher, Patricia, and Beverly Bentley. *Texas Women — Interviews and Images.* Austin: Shoal Creek Publishing, 1980 (104–109).
Loeddeke, Leslie. "Ninfa's Horizons Encompass 135 Restaurants." *Houston Chronicle,* September 8, 1981.
Personal biography of Ninfa Laurenzo.

Lydia Mendoza
Gil, Carlos. *The Houston Review,* Vol. 3, 1981.
Interview with Lydia Mendoza (with interpreter).
Texas Women's Hall of Fame. Texas Woman's University, Denton. 1986.

Irma Rangel
Crawford, Ann Fears, and Crystal Sasse Ragsdale. *Women in Texas.* Austin: Eakin Press, 1982.
Biographical material from Irma Rangel.
Telephone interview with Irma Rangel by Sammye Munson.

Tomás Rivera
Olivares, Julian, ed. *International Studies in Honor of Tomás Rivera.* Houston: Arte Publico Press, 1986.
Letters and papers from the Tomás Rivera Archive. University of California, Riverside.

Emma Tenayuca
Henderson, Richard. *Maury Maverick.* Austin: University of Texas Press, 1970 (214–219).
Rips, Geoffrey. "Living History: Emma Tenayuca Tells Her Story." *Texas Observer,* October 28, 1983.
Interview with Emma Tenayuca by Sammye Munson.

Felix and Janie Tijerina
Elliott, Keith. "Now Juanito Can Read." *Coronet,* July 1968.
Ewing, Betty. "Tijerina One Name That Means Civic-Mindedness." *Houston Chronicle,* July 14, 1986.
Grammer, Cleveland. "Success Didn't Come Easily for Restaurant Owner." *Houston Post,* July 27, 1986.
James, Ann. "Mrs. Felix Continues Husband's Work." *Houston Post,* June 1, 1967.
"A 400-word Start." *Time,* August 17, 1959.

Lee Trevino
Hopwood, Thomas. *Great Texans in Sports — The Immortals.* Fort Worth: Hopwood Productions, 1975.
Sports Illustrated, August 27, 1984.
Trevino, Lee, and Sam Blair. *They Call Me Super Mex.* New York: Random House, 1983.